Unit 2

Animal Discoveries

Mc
Graw
Hill
Education

Contents

At Home in Nome 1
short *o*, long *o*: *o_e*
Realistic Fiction: Diary

At Home in a Pond 7
short *o*, long *o*: *o_e*
Nonfiction

Duke and Bud's Run 11
short *u*, long *u*: *u_e*
Fable

Cute Cubs and Pups 19
short *u*, long *u*: *u_e*
Nonfiction

Animal Places and Spaces 23
soft *c*, soft *g*
Informational Text

Mice on Ice 31
soft *c*, soft *g*

Fiction

Baby Watch 35
ch, -tch, sh, ph, th, ng, wh

Informational Text

Phil the Chick 41
tch, -tch, sh, ph, th, ng, wh

Fiction

Mrs. Sprig's Spring Flowers 45
scr, shr, spl, spr, str, thr

Fantasy

A Thrilling Bird That Hums 53
scr, shr, spl, spr, str, thr

Nonfiction

At Home in Nome

May 9

I am in Nome. My family just moved here. I have a lot to tell. I have a big bed and not just a cot. I have a new school, too. I am scared because I do not know the kids. I hope they like me. I hope I make a lot of friends.

May 11

It is May, but it is still cold! Do not take off your hat. It is not hot like it is back home.

There were fox prints in the mud. Dad took a picture to take home.

May 15

Mom drove me to school. Back home I rode my bike. I like to ride.

All the kids spoke to me! I like my class. I made lots of friends. I will get to ride a big bus to school, too!

May 23

There are crab and cod in Nome.
I am glad I like cod. Yum! Yum!
Mom will make crab on the stove.
I hope I like it!

May 30

I will like making a trip back home
some time. I miss my pals. I miss
sitting in the sun. I miss running in the
grass. I miss riding a bike. But for now,
I am glad to have a home in Nome!

At Home in a Pond

A fish is at home in a big pond. It can swim home in a cave next to a cove. But, not all can swim alone.

7

Fish can swim in a big group. Fish swimming together is a school. It is like a family. Fish can swim, and It is safe.

Cod will not swim in a pond. Cod can not swim in a pond, but cod can swim in a school. Cod can swim next to rocks and stones. Cod will swim to get food. Cod can be safe in a big, big group.

Yes! Swim, cod, swim.

A lone fish is not safe. A school is
big. A lot of fish together can help
make it safe.

Duke and Bud's Run

On a June day, Bud the hare was sitting in the hot sun. "I bet I can win any race," Bud yelled. Bud could hop and run for miles and miles and miles. Bud was as fast as a man on a bike.

12

Duke the tortoise was sitting in the hot sun, too. He was up on a big hill in a tub of mud. Duke yelled to Bud, "I will race you. And I bet I will win because I am not rude like you. It is not wise to brag."

"Duke, you are funny," Bud said, "I have won five times. You will not win. I am fast! I am the best!"

"Yes, you and I should race," Duke said. "You are fast, but I am wise. Run and change, Bud."

Duke and Bud came to race at six. Bud had a big jug of water and a fan. Duke just had a bit of a smile.

Duke and Bud's friends came in time to see their race and cheer.

"Look," said Cal the cub. "I will tell you the rules. I will open the gate and hit a bell. You must run on the grass and not in the mud. Do not stop. To win, run up the hill and get to the red line.

Duke and Bud got set.

"Do not trip and fall," joked Bud.

"I hope you do well," said Duke.

Cal opened the gate. Bud ran off. He was fast. You could not spot him. Duke took his time, but he did not stop.

Bud stopped. He sat in the grass and hummed a tune. He sipped from his red jug. Bud even took a nap.

Duke did not go fast, but he did not stop. Bud woke up too late. Duke got to the red line and won! Bud was fuming.

Cute Cubs and Pups

Yes! Cubs and pups are cute,
cute, cute!

19

A cute cub is on a huge bit of ice. It will not fall! It is with its mom. Bears, lions and tigers are cubs. Cute cubs can have fun. Cubs jump up and run in mud and muck. Fun! Cubs will sit in the hot sun.

Small dogs are pups. Otters and seals are pups. Yes! Pups are cute. A pup just likes a soft rub. Rub a cute pup a lot! It is fun.

A pup is snug. It likes a hug. Yes! Moms of pups and cubs are huge. Pups and cubs are not huge yet. But trust us, they will get big.

CUTE PUPS	CUTE CUBS
seals	bears
otters	lions
dogs	tigers

Animal Places and Spaces

Animals make nice homes in many places and spaces.

This big wolf's home is a cave. The wolf has cubs in the cave. The cubs are safe there. Big cats and bats make fine homes in big caves too.

24

A mole lodges in the ground. It digs and digs making a hole it uses as its home. In a hole a mole gets food like grubs. A mole will pop straight out of a hole and show its face, but likes it best under the ground. It is safe there.

What animal makes a fine home
in a huge tree? A squirrel lives in
a tree. It can pull nuts off the tree.
A squirrel stuffs nuts in its face
making it bulge. A tree is a safe
place to hide and play.

A nest is a home for a bird. Birds use twigs, grass, and mud to make nests. Some nests look like cups. In a nest, birds can dodge enemies. Some birds will not budge if they are sitting on eggs. Birds can reuse a nest or make a new nest.

Index Stock/Alamy

A spider makes its home in a web. It spins a web. A web can get big. It is made out of silk. A web looks like lace you buy. You can dislike big spiders, but they trap bad bugs in their webs. Spiders dine on bugs.

Lots of animals make homes in water. Crabs and fish live in water almost as blue as the sky. Fish swim and dive in big waves. Some crabs move on and change homes. Some crabs wash up in hot sand.

29

On these pages you saw homes in lots of places and spaces. Caves, nests, and webs make nice homes.

Could an animal make a home in your home? Yes, a cage can make a nice home for some pets. Get a pet and make a home!

Animal	Home
wolf, cat, bat	cave
mole	hole
squirrel	tree
bird	nest
spider	web
crab, fish	water
pet	cage

Mice on Ice

In a place called Sage, a spot of water
froze on cement. It changed to ice. Now, it
was a nice ice rink just for mice!

Lots of mice came to skate on the frigid ice rink. It was a nice place. It was not big. The mice had lots of space to skate straight in a line, and it was a nice place to dance.

The nice mice ate food like rice and fudge. Some mice spent just a cent for a slice of cake. The mice had fun.

A big pigeon saw the ice rink. It
came and sat at the edge. It did not
budge.

"I am Stace, Can I skate?" she asked.

"Yes," the mice said. "Skate on ice. It
is fun!"

Baby Watch

Some baby animals can hatch from an egg. Some baby animals look like mom and dad. Some do not. These playful pups look like mom. Dog moms can have seven or eight pups at a time.

Stan Fellerman/Corbis

Early on, this baby will try to walk. Its long, thin legs shake, but it will start to run in just a bit. When this baby has to rest, it can take a nap while it is standing up.

This isn't a little baby. It is huge!
What can this big baby learn? It
can learn to use its long trunk. It
can grab food, get wet, and hang
on to a pal. When an elephant gets
hot, it is time for a long mud bath.
It likes that!

Some animal moms watch their babies. A little fish can make a nice lunch for a big fish. These baby fish swim close to mom. If one is in danger, it can rush and swim in to mom's mouth. It is safe there.

This cat is not in a big cage. Can you spot its face? Cubs hide while mom gets food. Mom can not chat with the cubs on a phone, but she can moan to get them. Cubs like running and playing, just like kids!

Phil the Chick

Phil the baby chick chipped at his shell. He did not get help. Then Phil hatched!

Phil sat in the shade to watch his Mom. "When can I learn things?" Phil asked. "I wish I could use my wings like Mom. I wish I was big like Mom. I want to try to do fun things like Mom."

Phil was thankful that he had such a nice Mom. Phil liked his Mom to sing to him.

"Cluck, cluck, cluck," she sang. Phil hoped to sing like his Mom, too.

But just to think about things made
Phil tired. It was such a big task to
hatch! Phil had to take a nap.

His Mom gazed at him and chanted,"
Cluck, Cluck, Cluck."

Mrs. Sprig's Spring Flowers

"When can I help?"
Chip asked.

"It is time, Chip," Mrs. Sprig
spoke up. "Move that dirt pile by
those far shrubs into this field."

Thad wished he could help, but
he was just too little.

"It is time to dig holes in this spot," said Mrs. Sprig with a smile.

Chip was strong. Chip dug and dug. He made a long strip of holes. Then Chip stopped to scratch his leg.

Thad just sat and watched.

"Next you must get this dirt wet," said Mrs. Sprig.

Chip grabbed a big hose. It was fun making water splish and splash until the dirt was ready. It looked like mud.

Thad *really* wished he could help.

Mrs. Sprig had packs of strange little seeds. "I like lots and lots of spring flowers," she said.

"Thad, you are just the right size for this fun job. Shake seeds in the holes just like this," Mrs. Sprig said.

Thad was thrilled to pitch in.

Mrs. Sprig said, "This seed will grow into a blue flower. It will need light and water. Then you will see leaves spring up. This seed will grow into a big orange and white flower."

Bird stopped to sit and chat.

"Bird, it is nice that you came.
I like your red hat," said Mrs. Sprig.

"We are done planting. We will
scrub up and change. Then you
can have pie with us."

Mrs. Sprig, Chip, Thad, and Bird sat in the sun and had pie. Chip ate a little slice, and Thad ate a big slice!

Mrs. Sprig sat back and pictured a flowerbed filled with lots and lots of spring flowers.

A Thrilling Bird That Hums

Check the next 3 pages for splendid and thrilling facts.

Yuqun Cao/iStock/Getty Images Plus/Getty Images

A hummingbird is a small bird. It can flap its wings wide and fast. It can zip, zip, zip. It flaps its wings fast and makes a fun hum, hum, hum.

Larry Keller, Lititz Pa./Moment Open/Getty Images

This bird has a splendid red neck. Its bill is like a long straw. It pokes its bill inside flowers and gets food. It likes bugs, too. It will not go home until it gets its food.

Robert Harnden/iStock/Getty Images

What Is It?

This is not a hummingbird! It is a nice moth. Do not confuse it. It will not scratch. Is this insect strange or thrilling? Is this insect splendid? It is a fake hummingbird, that makes it safe.

At Home in Nome   WORD COUNT: 210

DECODABLE WORDS
Target Phonics Elements
   Short o*: cod, cot, hot, fox, lot, lots, Mom, not, on
   Long o: o_e*: home, Nome, hope, drove, rode, spoke, stove

HIGH-FREQUENCY WORDS
because, cold, family, friends, have, know, off, picture, school, took
Review: all, are, do, here, like, me, move, my, new, of, show, some, the, there, they, to, too, were, your
Story Words: May, back, scared

At Home in a Pond   WORD COUNT: 124

DECODABLE WORDS
Target Phonics Elements
   Short o*: cod, lot, not, pond, rocks
   Long o: o_e*: alone, cove, home, stones

HIGH-FREQUENCY WORDS
family, know, school
Review: all, are, by, help, little, make, of, their, the, these, they, to
Story Words: fish, food, group

Duke and Bud's Run   WORD COUNT: 313

DECODABLE WORDS
Target Phonics Elements
   Short u*: Bud, but, funny, hummed, jug, just, must, run, sun, up
   Long u: u_e*: Duke, June, rude, rules, tune

HIGH-FREQUENCY WORDS
cheer, change, fall, five, look, open, should, their, won, yes
Review: any, are, because, could, do, even, for, funny, have, he, of, open, said, see, the, to, too, took, was, water, you
Story Words: day, hare, race, tortoise

Cute Cubs and Pups   WORD COUNT: 127

DECODABLE WORDS
Target Phonics Elements
   Short u*: but, chunk, cub, cubs, fun, hug, hunt, jump, just, mud, muck, rub, run, snug, sun, pup, pups, up
   Long u: u_e*: cute, huge

HIGH-FREQUENCY WORDS
fall, look, yes
Review: and, are, have, little, of, so, small, the, they
Story Words: bears, lions, otters, seals, tigers

Previously Taught

Animal Places and Spaces

DECODABLE WORDS
Target Phonics Elements
Soft c*: face, lace, nice, place, places, spaces
Soft g*; dge*: budge, dodge, lodges; **ge***: huge, pages, cage; **lge***: bulge; **nge***: change

HIGH-FREQUENCY WORDS
almost, buy, food, out, pull, saw, sky, straight, under, wash
Review: are, change, could, for, look, move, new, of, or, play, show, some, the, their, there, they, this, to, too, water, what, you, your
Story Words: animal(s), birds, blue, enemies, fish, ground, live(s), squirrel, spiders, these, tree

---

Mice on Ice

DECODABLE WORDS
Target Phonics Elements
Soft c*: cement, cent, city, ice, mice, place, rice, slice, space, Stace
Soft g*; dge* : budge, edge, fudge; **g***: frigid, Sage

HIGH-FREQUENCY WORDS
food, saw, sky
Review: for, of, said, she, some, the, to, was, water
Story Words: pigeon

Baby Watch

DECODABLE WORDS
Target Phonics Elements
Consonant Digraphs; ch*: chat, lunch; **–tch***: hatch, watch; **sh***: fish, rush, shake; **ph***: elephant, phone; **th***: that, the, their, them, there, these, thin, this; **ng***: long, hang; **wh***: what, when, while

HIGH-FREQUENCY WORDS
baby, early, eight, isn't, learn, seven, start, these, try, walk
Review: food, for, from, have, little, look, one, or, she, some, the, their, there, they, to, you
Story Words: animal(s), babies, danger, elephant, moan, mouth, watch

Previously Taught

Phil the Chick

DECODABLE WORDS
Target Phonics Elements
Consonant Digraphs: *ch**: chanted, chipped, chick, such; *–tch**: hatch, hatched, watch; *sh**: shade, shell, wish; *ph**: Phil; *th**: thankful, then, the, think, things, *ng**: sang, sing, wings, *wh**: when

HIGH-FREQUENCY WORDS
baby, learn, try
Review: about, could, he, my, she, the, to, too, want

---

eek 5 | **Mrs. Sprig's Spring Flowers**

WORD COUNT: 288

DECODABLE WORDS
Target Phonics Elements
Three-Letter Blends; *scr-**: scratch, scrub; *shr-**: shrubs; *spl-**: splash, splish; *spr-**: Sprig, Sprig's, spring; *str-**: strip, strong, strange; *thr-**: thrilled

HIGH-FREQUENCY WORDS
bird, far, field, flower, grow, leaves, light, orange, ready, until
Review: are, by, could, done, for, have, he, into, little, looked, move, of, pictured, right, said, see, she, the, to, too, was, water, you
Story Words: dirt, need, pie, really, seed(s), we

A Thrilling Bird That Hums

WORD COUNT: 124

DECODABLE WORDS
Target Phonics Elements
Three-Letter Blends *scr-**: scratch; *str-*: strange; *thr-*: thrilling; *spl-*: splendid

HIGH-FREQUENCY WORDS
bird, far, flowers, until
Review: do, go, small, the, too
Story Words: bird, food, hummingbird, moth

Previously Taught

59

HIGH FREQUENCY WORDS

Grade K
a
and
are
can
come
do
does
for
go
good
has
have
he
help
here
I
is
like
little
look
me
my
of
play
said
see
she
the
they
this
to
too
want
was
we
what
where
who
with
you

Grade 1
about
above
after
again
ago
all
animal
another

answer
any
around
away
be
been
before
began
better
blue
boy
brother
brought
build
busy
buy
by
call
carry
caught
children
climb
color
come
could
day
does
done
door
down
early
eat
eight
enough
every
eyes
fall
father
favorite
few
find
flew
food
found
four
friend
from
front
full
fun
girl

give
gone
good
great
green
grow
guess
happy
hard
heard
help
her
how
instead
into
jump
knew
know
large
laugh
learn
listen
live
love
make
many
money
month
more
mother
move
near
new
no
none
not
nothing
now
of
oh
old
once
one
only
or
other
our
out
over
people
picture

place
poor
pretty
pull
push
put
question
right
round
run
school
should
small
so
some
soon
start
sure
surprise
their
then
there
they
thought
three
through
today
together
tomorrow
too
toward
two
under
up
upon
very
use
walk
want
warm
water
way
were
what
who
why
woman
wonder
work
would
write

year
young
your

Grade 2
all
almost
and
another
any
are
baby
ball
because
bird
blue
both
boy
buy
by
change
cheer
cold
could
do
done
early
eight
even
fall
family
far
field
find
five
flower
food
for
friends
funny
girl
go
goes
green
grow
has
have
he
help
here
how
into
isn't
know

learn
leaves
light
like
little
look
me
move
my
new
now
number
of
off
on
one
open
or
orange
other
out
picture
play
pull
put
ready
right
said
saw
says
school
see
seven
she
should
show
sky
small
some
sounds
start
straight
the
their
there
they
this
to
too
took
try
under
understands
until

walk
want
was
wash
water
were
what
where
why
won
work
year
yellow
yes
you
your

DECODING SKILLS TAUGHT TO DATE

short *a, i; -s, -es* (plural nouns); short *e, o, u; -s, -es* (inflectional endings); two-letter blends: *r*-blends, *s*-blends, *t*-blends, *l*-blends; closed syllables; short *a*, long *a: a_e; -ed, -ing* (inflectional endings); short *i*, long *i: i_e;* possessives; short *o*, long *o: o_e;* short *u*, long *u: u_e; -ed, -ing* (w/ doubling final consonants; drop final *e*); CVCe syllables; soft *c* and *g: dge, ge, lge, nge, rge;* prefixes *re-, un-, dis-;* consonant digraphs: *ch, -tch, sh, ph, th, ng, wh;* suffixes *-ful, -less;* three-letter blends: *scr, spr, str, thr, spl, shr;* compound words